God could not be everywhere, so He made mothers.

Jewish Proverb

This 1998 edition exclusive to

(714) 587-9207

Printed in China. ISBN 1-85081-080-X

Mothers

a collection of poetry and prose
in celebration of mothers

There is only one pretty child in the world,
and every mother has it.

Chinese Proverb

fit for Heaven

Mother is the name for God in the lips and hearts of little children.

W. M. Thackeray

G od knows how infantine the memory may have been, that was awakened within me by the sound of my mother's voice in the old parlour, when I set foot in the hall. She was singing in a low tone. I think I must have lain in her arms, and heard her singing so to me when I was but a baby. The strain was new to me, and yet it was so old that it filled my heart brimful, like a friend come back from a long absence.

I believed, from the solitary and thoughtful way in which my mother murmured her song, that she was alone. And I went softly into the room. She was sitting by the fire, suckling an infant, whose tiny hand she held against her neck. Her eyes were looking down upon its face, and she sat singing to it. I was so far right, that she had no other companion.

I spoke to her, and she started, and cried out. But seeing me, she called me her dear Davy, her own boy! and coming half across the room to meet me, kneeled down upon the ground and kissed me, and laid my head down on her bosom near the little creature that was nestling there, and put its hand up to my lips.

I wish I had died. I wish I had died then, with that feeling in my heart! I should have been more fit for Heaven than I ever have been since.

from David Copperfield by Charles Dickens

— 9 —

We find delight in the beauty and happiness of children that makes the heart too big for the body.

Ralph Waldo Emerson

'**M**other, do you have "plans," as Mrs. Moffat said?' asked Meg, bashfully.

'Yes, my dear, I have a great many; all mothers do, but mine differ somewhat from Mrs. Moffat's, I suspect. . . .

'I want my daughters to be beautiful, accomplished, and good; to be admired, loved, and respected; to have a happy youth, to be well and wisely married, and to lead useful, pleasant lives, with as little care and sorrow to try them as God sees fit to send. To be loved and chosen by a good man is the best and sweetest thing which can happen to a woman; and I sincerely hope my girls may know this beautiful experience. It is natural to think of it, Meg; right to hope and wait for it, and wise to prepare for it; so that, when the happy time comes, you may feel ready for the duties, and worthy of the joy. My dear girls, I am ambitious for you, but not to have you make a dash in the world—marry rich men merely because they are rich, or have splendid houses, which are not homes because love is wanting. Money is a needful and precious thing—and, when well used, a noble thing—but I never want you to think of it as the first or only prize to strive for. I'd rather see you poor men's wives, if you were happy, beloved, contented, than queens on thrones, without self-respect and peace.

'One thing remember, my girls; mother is always ready to be your confidante, father to be your friend; and both of us trust and hope that our daughters, whether married or single, will be the pride and comfort of our lives.'

from Little Women by Louisa M Alcott

the pride and comfort of our lives

Stories first heard at a mother's knee are never wholly forgotten – a little spring that never quite dries up in our journey through scorching years.

Giovanni Ruffini

A Grandmother's Love . . .

'If I could have kept the dear child, without the dread that's always upon me of his coming to that fate I have spoken of, I could never have parted with him, even to you. For I love him, I love him, I love him. I love my husband long dead and gone, in him; I love my children dead and gone, in him; I love my young and hopeful days dead and gone, in him. I couldn't sell that love, and look in your bright face. It's a free gift.'

from Our Mutual Friend by Charles Dickens

Who is it that loves me and will love me for ever with an affection which no chance, no misery, no crime of mine can do away? It is you, my mother.

Thomas Carlyle

There is in all this cold and hollow world no fount of deep, strong, deathless love, save that within a mother's heart.

Felicia D. Hemans

James James
Morrison Morrison
Weatherby George Dupree
Took great
Care of his Mother
Though he was only three.

A A Milne

He had come back to his mother. Hers was the strongest tie in his life. ... And nobody else mattered. There was one place in the world that stood solid and did not melt into unreality: the place where his mother was. Everybody else could grow shadowy, almost non-existent to him, but she could not. It was as if the pivot and pole of his life, from which he could not escape, was his mother.

And in the same way she waited for him. In him was established her life now. ... She saw that our chance for doing is here, and doing counted with her. Paul was going to prove that she had been right; he was going to make a man whom nothing should shift off his feet; he was going to alter the face of the earth in some way which mattered. Wherever he went she felt her soul went with him. Whatever he did, she felt her soul stood by him, ready, as it were, to hand him his tools. ...

And he came back to her. And in his soul was a feeling of the satisfaction of self-sacrifice because he was faithful to her. She loved him first; he loved her first.

from Sons and Lovers by D H Lawrence

Every baby born into the world is a finer one than the last.
Charles Dickens: Nicholas Nickleby

angels whispering

In the heavens above
The angels, whispering to one another,
Can find, amid their burning terms of love,
None so devotional as that of 'mother'.

Edgar Allen Poe

So for the mother's sake the child was dear,
And dearer was the mother for the child.

Samuel Taylor Coleridge

Youth fades; love droops; the leaves of friendship fall:
A mother's secret love outlives them all.

Oliver Wendell Holmes

A Cradle Song

Sweet dreams for a shade,
O'er my lovely infant's head.
Sweet dreams of pleasant streams.
By happy silent moony beams.

Sweet sleep with soft down,
Weave thy brows an infant crown.
Sweet sleep Angel mild,
Hover o'er my happy child.

Sweet smiles in the night,
Hover over my delight.
Sweet smiles, Mother's smiles
All the livelong night beguiles.

Sweet moans, dovelike sighs,
Chase not slumber from thy eyes.
Sweet moans, sweeter smiles.
All the doverlike moans beguiles.

Sleep sleep happy child.
All creation slept and smil'd.
Sleep sleep, happy sleep.
While o'er thee thy mother weep.

William Blake

A mother has, perhaps, the hardest earthly lot; and yet no mother worthy of the name ever gave herself thoroughly for her child who did not feel that, after all, she reaped what she had sown.

Henry Ward Beecher

the hardest earthly lot

The joys of parents are secret, and so are their griefs and fears:
they cannot utter the one, nor they will not utter the other.

Francis Bacon

Mrs. Darling first heard of Peter when she was tidying up her children's minds. It is the nightly custom of every good mother after her children are asleep to rummage in their minds and put things straight for next morning, repacking into their proper places the many articles that have wandered during the day. If you could keep awake (but of course you can't) you would see your own mother doing this, and you would find it very interesting to watch her. It is quite like tidying up drawers. You would see her on her knees, I expect, lingering humorously over some of your contents, wondering where on earth you had picked this thing up, making discoveries sweet and not so sweet, pressing this to her cheek as if it were as nice as a kitten, and hurriedly stowing that out of sight. When you wake in the morning, the naughtinesses and evil passions with which you went to bed have been folded up small and placed at the bottom of your mind; and on the top, beautifully aired, are spread out your prettier thoughts, ready for you to put on.

from Peter Pan by J M Barrie

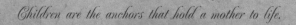

Children are the anchors that hold a mother to life.

Sophocles

Many people have said to me
'What a pity you had such a big family
to raise. Think of the novels and the
short stories and the poems you never
had time to write because of that.'
And I looked at my children and I said,
'These are my poems. These are my
short stories.'

Olga Masters

A happy childhood is one of the best gifts that parents
have it in their power to bestow.

Mary Cholmondeley

The best thing you can give children,
next to good habits, are good memories.

Sydney J Harris

Only a mother knows a mother's fondness.

Lady Mary Wortley Montagu

I remember my mother's prayers and they have followed me.
They have clung to me all my life.

Abraham Lincoln

Song

Oh, baby, baby, baby dear,
We lie alone together here;
The snowy gown and cap and sheet
With lavender are fresh and sweet;
Through half-closed blinds the roses peer
To see and love you, baby dear.

We are so tired, we like to lie
Just doing nothing, you and I
Within the darkened quiet room.
The sun sends dusk rays through the gloom,
Which is no gloom since you are here,
My little life, my baby dear.

Soft sleepy mouth so vaguely pressed
Against your new-made mother's breast,
Soft little hands in mine I fold,
Soft little feet I kiss and hold,
Round soft smooth head and tiny ear,
All mine, my own, my baby dear.

And he we love is far away!
But he will come some happy day,
You need but me, and I can rest
At peace with you beside me pressed.
There are no questions, longings vain,
No murmurings, nor doubt, nor pain,
Only content and we are here,
My baby dear.

Edith Nesbit

all mine, my own

Cornelia, the mother of the Gracchi, once
entertained a woman from Campania at her house.
Since the woman made a great show of her jewels,
which were among the most beautiful of the time,
Cornelia detained her conversation until her
children came home from school.
Then, pointing to her children, she said,
'These are my jewels.'

Valerius Maximus

these are my jewels

There is an enduring tenderness in the love of a mother. . . .
It is neither to be chilled by selfishness, nor daunted by danger, . . .
She will sacrifice every comfort to his convenience; she will
surrender every pleasure to his enjoyment; she will glory in his
fame and exalt in his prosperity; and if adversity overtake him,
he will be the dearer to her by misfortune; and if disgrace settle
upon his name, she will still love and cherish him; and if all the
world beside cast him off, she will be all the world to him.

Washington Irving

There's no vocabulary
For love within a family,
ove that's lived in
But not looked at,
love within the light of which
All else is seen, the love within which
All other love finds speech.
This love is silent.

T S Eliot

Children are the true connoisseurs.
What's precious to them has no price, only value.

Bel Kaufman

I shall never forget my mother, for it was she who planted and nurtured the first seeds of good within me. She opened my heart to the lasting impressions of nature; she awakened my understanding and extended my horizon and her percepts exerted an everlasting influence upon the course of my life.

Immanuel Kant

My Mother

Who fed me from her gentle breast,
And hushed me in her arms to rest,
And on my cheek sweet kisses prest?
My Mother.

When pain and sickness made me cry,
Who gazed upon my heavy eye,
And wept, for fear that I should die?
My Mother.

Who dressed my doll in clothes so gay,
And fondly taught me how to play,
And minded all I had to say?
My Mother.

Who ran to help me when I fell,
And would some pretty story tell,
Or kiss the place to make it well?
My Mother.

And can I ever cease to be
Affectionate and kind to thee,
Who was so very kind to me?
My Mother.

Anne Taylor

who ran to help?

Womanliness means only motherhood;
All love begins and ends there.

Robert Browning

A babe in a house is a well-spring
of pleasure, a messenger of
peace and love.

Martin Farquhar Tupper

The best academy, a mother's knee.

James Russell Lowell

'Yes, Jo, I think your harvest will be a good one,' began Mrs. March. . . .

'Not half so good as yours, mother. Here it is, and we never can thank you enough for the patient sowing and reaping you have done,' cried Jo, with the loving impetuosity which she never could outgrow.

'I hope there will be more wheat and fewer tares every year,' said Amy softly.

'A large sheaf, but I know there's room in your heart for it, Marmee dear,' added Meg's tender voice.

Touched to the heart, Mrs. March could only stretch out her arms, as if to gather children and grand-children to herself, and say, with face and voice full of motherly love, gratitude, and humility:

'Oh, my girls, however long you may live, I never can wish you a greater happiness than this!'

from Good Wives by Louisa M Alcott

Children are the hands by which we take hold of heaven.

Henry Ward Beecher

love and tenderness

Fifty-four years of love and tenderness and crossness and devotion and
unswerving loyalty. Without her I could have achieved a quarter of
what I have achieved, not only in terms of success and career, but in
terms of personal happiness. . . . She has never stood between me and
my life, never tried to hold me too tightly, always let me go free . . .

Noel Coward

My mother was the making of me. She was so true and so sure of me, I felt that I had someone to live for – someone I must not disappoint. The memory of my mother will always be a blessing to me.

Thomas A Edison

My mother was the most beautiful woman. . . . All I am I owe to my mother. . . . I attribute all my success in life to the moral, intellectual and physical education I received from her.

George Washington

A mother is a mother still,
The holiest thing alive.

Samuel Taylor Coleridge

The future destiny of the child
is always the work of the mother.

Napoleon Bonaparte

They say that man is mighty,
He governs land and sea,
He wields a mighty sceptre,
O'er lesser powers that be,
But a mightier power and stronger,
Man from his throne has hurled,
For the hand that rocks the cradle,
Is the hand that rocks the world.

William Ross Wallace

the hand that rocks the cradle

given by God

'No one loves me, –
no one cares for me, but you, mother.'

He turned away and stood leaning his head against the mantelpiece, tears forcing themselves into his manly eyes. She stood up, – she tottered. For the first time in her life, the strong woman tottered. She put her hands on his shoulders; she was a tall woman. She looked into his face; she made him look at her.

'Mother's love is given by God, John. It holds fast for ever and ever.'

from North and South by Elizabeth Gaskell

for ever and ever

Acknowledgements

Pg 5 Mothely Love by Gustave-Leonhard de Jonghe (1828-93), Berko Fine Paintings, Knokke-Zoute /Bridgeman Art Library, London; pg 6 Motherhood, 1898 by Louis (Emile) Adan (1839-1937), Waterhouse and Dodd, London/Bridgeman Art Library, London; pg 7 A Mother and her Small Children by Edith Hume (fl. 1862-92), Josef Mensing Gallery, Hamm-Rhynern/Bridgeman Art Library, London; pg 8 Mrs Masarai and her Daugher, 1896 by Hans Tichy (1861-1925), Private Collection/Bridgeman Art Library, London; pg 10-11 The Dancing Bear by Frederick Morgan (1856-1927), Roy Miles Gallery, 29 Bruton Street, London/Bridgeman Art Library London; pg 13 A Fairy Tale by Carlton Alfred Smith (1853-1946), Towneley Hall Art Gallery & Museum, Burnley/Bridgeman Art Library, London; pg 14 Mother and Child by Charles James Lewis (1830-92), Christopher Wood Gallery, London/Bridgeman Art Library, London; pg 15 An Introduction by Emily Crawford (1869-91), Christopher Wood Gallery, London/Bridgeman Art Library, London; pg 16 The Little Accident by Antal Neogrady (1861-1942), Berko Fine Paintings, Knokke-Zoute/Bridgeman Art Library, London; pg 17 Mother and Child in a Wooded Landscape, 1913 by Harold Harvey (1874-1941), Gavin Graham Gallery, London/Bridgeman Art Library, London; pg 18 Mother and Son by Fritz Zuber-Buhler (1822-1896), Christie's, London/Bridgeman Art Library; pg 20 The New Baby by Evert Pieters (1856-1932), Private Collection/Bridgeman Art Library, London; pg 21 Lullaby by Robert Gemmel Hutchinson (1855-1936)), Sotheby's Picture Library; pg 22 A Mother's Darling, 1880, by Jessie McGregor D.1919, Sotheby's Picture Library; pg 24 A Morning Nap by Carlton Alfred Smith (1853-1946), Sotheby's Picture Library; pg 25 The Newborn Child by Theodore Gerard (1829-95), Private Collection/Bridgeman Art Library, London; pg 26 The First, the only one by John Haynes-Williams (1836-1908), York City Art Gallery/Bridgeman Art Library, London; pg 27 Sweet Dreams by Thomas Brooks (1818-91), Phillips, The International Fine Art Auctioneers/Bridgeman Art Library, London; pg 29 Mother and Baby by Dutch School, (19th Century), Josef Mensing Gallery, Hamm-Rhynern/Bridgeman Art Library, London; pg 30-31 The Bleaching Ground by Friedrich Edouard Meyerheim (1808-79), Josef Mensing Gallery, Hamm-Rhynern/Bridgeman Art Library, London; pg 32 On the Beach by Eugene De Blaas (1843-1931), Sotheby's Picture Library; pg 34 Breakfast Time by Norman Hepple (1908-1994), Bonhams, London/Bridgeman Art Library, London; pg 35 Undressing the Baby by Johann Georg Meyer von Bremen (1813-86), Josef Mensing Gallery, Hamm-Rhynern/Bridgeman Art Library, London; pg 36 Maternity by Beatrice Howe (20th century), Atkinson Art Gallery, Southport, Lancs./Bridgeman Art Library, London; pg 37 Mother & Child, 1901 by English School, (20th Century), Warrington Museum & Art Gallery, Lancs./Brigeman Art Library, London; pg 39 The Mother by Thomas Musgrave Joy (1812-66), York City Art Gallery/Bridgeman Art Library, London; pg 40 Maternity by Thomas Benjamin Kennington (1856-1916), Sotheby's Picture Library; pg 42-43 Helping Mother by Giovanni Battista Torrigia (b.1858), Christies, London/Bridgeman Art Library, London; pg 44 The New Brood by Alfred Provis (fl.1843-86), Hampshire Gallery, Bournemouth/Bridgeman Art Library, London; pg 45 Mother and Child, 1880, by William Oliver (1867-1882), Sotheby's Picture Library; pg 46 Maternal Care by Evert Pieters (1856-1932), Josef Mensing Gallery, Hamm-Rhynern/Bridgeman Art Library, London; pg 47 The Happy Mother by Antoine de Bruycker (1816-84), Josef Mensing Gallery, Hamm-Rhynern/Bridgeman Art Library, London; pg 48-49 The First Tooth by Frederick Morgan (1856-1927), Sotheby's Picture Library; pg 50 Mother and Baby by George Smith (1783-1869), John Noott Galleries, Boradway, Worcs./Bridgeman Art Library, London; pg 51 Springtime, Feeding the Lambs by Frederick Morgan (1856-1927), Sotheby's Picture Library; pg 53 Out of Reach, Daughers of Eve, 1895 (w/c) by Sir Frank Dicksee (1853-1928), Chris Beetles Ltd., London/Bridgeman Art Library, London; pg 54 Collecting May Blossom by Thomas P Hall (fl.1837-67), Eaton Gallery, Princes Arcade, London/Bridgeman Art Library, London; pg 57 Baby'sBirthday by Frederick Daniel Hardy (1826-1911), Wolverhampton Art Gallery & Museum, Staffs/Bridgeman Art Library, London; pg 58 The Cradle, 1872 by Berthe Morisot (1841-95), Musee d'Orsay, Paris/Bridgeman Art Library; pg 59 'Angel and Devil' or 'Playing Diabolo, The Devil-on-two-Sticks' 1868 by Cesare Felix dell' Acqua (1821-1925), Berko Fine Paintings, Knokke-Soute/Bridgeman Art Library, London; pg 60 My Lady is a Widow and Childless by Marcus Stone (1840-1920), Forbes Magazine Collection, New York/Bridgeman Art Library, London

Other images © Robert Frederick Ltd. 1996